POURQUOI STORIES

BY
VIRGINIA
LOH-HAGAN

People have been telling stories since the beginning of time. This series focuses on stories found across cultures. You may have heard these stories from your parents or grandparents. Or you may have told one yourself around a campfire. Stories explain the world around us. They inspire. They motivate. They even scare! We tell stories to share our history.

45th Parallel Press

Published in the United States of America by Cherry Lake Publishing
Ann Arbor, Michigan
www.cherrylakepublishing.com

Reading Adviser: Marla Conn MS, Ed., Literacy specialist, Read-Ability, Inc.
Book Designer: Jen Wahi

Photo Credits: ©Viorel Sima/Shutterstock.com, 5; ©SusaImages/Shutterstock.com, 7; ©Mriya Wildlife/Shutterstock.com, 8; Mumemories/Shutterstock.com, 11; ©Catmando/Shutterstock.com, 13; ©Ronnie Howard/Shutterstock.com, 14; ©Zadiraka Evgenii/Shutterstock.com, 17; ©DR-images/Shutterstock.com, 19; ©Jeff McGraw/Shutterstock.com, 21; ©anekoho/Shutterstock.com, 23; ©Brandt Bolding/Shutterstock.com, 25; ©Maksimilian/Shutterstock.com, 27; ©Dirk M. de Boer/Shutterstock.com, 28; ©FlavoredPixels/Shutterstock.com, cover and interior; Various grunge/texture patterns throughout courtesy of Shutterstock.com

45th Parallel Press is an imprint of Cherry Lake Publishing.

Library of Congress Cataloging-in-Publication Data

Names: Loh-Hagan, Virginia, author.
Title: Pourquoi stories / by Virginia Loh-Hagan.
Description: [Ann Arbor : Cherry Lake Publishing, 2019] | Series: Stone circle stories. Culture and folktales | Includes bibliographical references and index.
Identifiers: LCCN 2018035177| ISBN 9781534143500 (hardcover) | ISBN 9781534140066 (pbk.) | ISBN 9781534141261 (pdf) | ISBN 9781534142466 (hosted ebook)
Subjects: | CYAC: Nature--Folklore. | Folklore.
Classification: LCC PZ8.1.L936 Pou 2019 | DDC [398.2]--dc23
LC record available at https://lccn.loc.gov/2018035177

Printed in the United States of America
Corporate Graphics

ABOUT THE AUTHOR:

Dr. Virginia Loh-Hagan is an author, university professor, and former classroom teacher. She wonders why she can't lose weight. She lives in San Diego with her very tall husband and very naughty dogs. To learn more about her, visit www.virginialoh.com.

TABLE OF CONTENTS

POURQUOI STORIES

What is a pourquoi story?
How is it different from a creation story?
Why are pourquoi stories important?

Pourquoi is a French word. It means "why." Pourquoi stories explain why something is the way it is. An example is why dogs bark. Pourquoi stories are different from creation stories. Creation stories explain how the universe was created.

Before science, people wondered about the world. They made up stories. These stories explained nature. They explained how the world worked. They helped people understand things. Today, people have science to explain things.

Many cultures have pourquoi tales.

But pourquoi stories still give us a lot of information. They help us learn more about people who lived long ago. They give us information about their beliefs.

CHAPTER 1

WHY LIZARDS CAN'T SIT UPRIGHT

Where did this story come from?
How is the magical otter a good friend?
What does the husband learn?

Brer means brother. Brer Rabbit and his animal friends are popular characters. They come from African stories. African **slaves** brought these stories to the United States. Slaves are people who are forced to work.

I like to keep a low profile.

Lizards are reptiles. They have small heads, long bodies, and long tails.

A long time ago, Brer Lizard looked a lot like Brer Frog. He also sat like a dog. He could sit **upright**. Upright means having a straight back.

Brer Lizard and Brer Frog were friends. They did many things together. One day, they got bored. They went on a walk. They looked ahead. They saw something wonderful. They saw a big pond. They got excited.

Brer Lizard said, "Wow! It looks great over there. We can catch bugs. We can eat all we want."

Frogs have long back legs and webbed feet. This helps them jump and swim.

Brer Frog looked at the sparkling water. He said, "We can also go swimming."

They ran as fast as they could. But there was a problem. There was a big fence in their way. This made them sad. Brer Lizard said, "The fence is too high. We can't jump over it."

Brer Frog said, "The fence is too deep in the ground. We can't dig under it."

Brer Lizard said, "It's too far to walk around the fence."

Then, Brer Frog saw a small crack in the fence. The crack was low to the ground. Brer Frog said, "I'm going to squeeze through. Help me!" He pushed. He shoved. He got through the crack. He popped out to the other side. He yelled over to Brer Lizard. He said, "Brer Lizard, come on over. It's great over here."

Brer Lizard was jealous. He said, "I'm coming! I'm also going to squeeze through." He pushed. He shoved. But a part of the fence fell. It fell on top of Brer Lizard. It smashed him flat. After that, Brer Lizard couldn't sit upright any more. He also never got to the pond. That's why lizards can't sit upright.

The story's lesson is to not take shortcuts.

CHAPTER 2

HOW BEAVER GOT HIS TAIL

What happened to Beaver's tail?
Where did this story come from?
What did Beaver learn?

The Ojibwe are Native Americans. They're from the Great Lakes area. This is near Michigan.

A long time ago, there was Beaver. In the beginning, Beaver had a big, fluffy tail. He loved to **brag** about his tail. Brag means to show off. One day, Beaver went on a walk. He stopped to talk to Bird. He said, "Don't you wish your feathers were as beautiful as my tail?"

Bird rolled his eyes. He said, "Why do you think so much of your tail?'"

12

The Ojibwe were mainly hunters and fishermen.

Beaver was upset. He walked away. He stopped to drink at the river. He ran into Otter. He said, "Don't you wish your fur was as beautiful as my tail?"

Otter said, "Not really." He walked away.

Beaver said, "How rude." He was upset. He decided to spend his energy building a new **dam**. Dams are barriers. They hold back water. They're also beaver homes.

I've always wanted a home by the water.

Beavers build dams to create pools of water.

Beaver cut down logs. While cutting, he thought about his tail. He didn't pay attention. He cut the tree in the wrong way. The tree fell toward him. Beaver jumped. But he didn't jump fast enough. The tree fell on his tail.

Beaver pulled. He tugged. He finally got his tail from under the log. When he saw his tail, he cried. He said, "Oh no! My beautiful tail. It's flat!" He cried and cried.

The **Creator** is a being who made the world. He asked, "Why are you crying?"

FAST-FORWARD TO MODERN TIMES

It's hard to trace a folktale's beginnings. But we know how the Johnny Kaw legend got started. Kaw was created in 1955. He's admired as a Kansas folk hero. He was created by George Fillinger. Fillinger was a professor at Kansas State University. He created Kaw to celebrate the 100th birthday of Manhattan, Kansas. He wanted people to be interested in Kansas history. His stories were first printed in a local newspaper. The Johnny Kaw legend grew. Other books were written about him. Art was done of him. A statue of him is in a city park. The statue is 30 feet (9 meters) tall. Kaw was amazing. He played in the Missouri River. He sat down. His rear end made a valley. He built the Rocky Mountains and the Grand Canyon. He planted wheat, sunflowers, and big potatoes. He created tornadoes. He twisted clouds to make rain. His pets were a wildcat and jayhawk. His pets liked to fight. This created the Dust Bowl. Kaw fought with Paul Bunyan. He made the Mississippi River by dragging Bunyan's face in the ground.

Beaver said, "A tree has smashed my beautiful tail. Now, no one will like me."

The Creator said, "Others don't care about your tail. They care if you're kind and wise."

Beaver said, "But it's so ugly!"

The Creator said, "Your tail is more useful now. It can hold you up while you sit. It can help you swim faster. It can help you warn others. Just slap your tail on the water."

This made Beaver happy. Beaver stopped bragging about his tail. He helped others. The other animals liked him better. That's how Beaver got a flat tail.

Beaver tails can grow to be 15 inches (38 centimeters) long and 6 inches (15 cm) wide.

CHAPTER 3

HOW THUNDER AND LIGHTNING CAME TO BE

How were thunder and lightning created?
Where did this story come from?
What lessons are taught in this story?

Inuit are Native Americans. They're from Alaska, northern Canada, and Greenland.

A long time ago, there was a big party. People celebrated the coming of spring. They danced. They sang. They ate a lot. Almost everyone was happy. Two people were sad. They were brother and sister. The girl was 2 years older than the boy.

This story is also called "The Legend of Lightning and Thunder."

They were **orphans**. Orphans are children whose parents have died.

The orphans traveled far to get to the party. But the food ran out. The orphans didn't get any food. They were hungry. They were willing to do anything for food.

CROSS-CULTURAL CONNECTION

There is a popular folktale from Vietnam. It's about how Tiger got his stripes. Tiger was proud of his beautiful golden coat. He saw Buffalo working in a field. He said, "Buffalo, why are you working for that man? You are bigger and stronger than him." Buffalo said, "Man has wisdom." Tiger wanted wisdom. He went to Man. He said, "Give me your wisdom." Man didn't want to do that. He tricked Tiger. He said, "I left my wisdom at home. I will go get it. But wait for me. Let me tie you to this tree. You can help me watch my buffalo." Tiger agreed. Man came back. He brought back straw. He set it on fire under Tiger. He said, "This is my wisdom." Tiger tried to escape. He burned his coat. He escaped. He ran to the river. The orange stripes are the flames. The black stripes are the ropes. That's how Tiger got his stripes!

The girl said, "We need to steal food."

The boy knew stealing was wrong. But he obeyed his sister.

The orphans stole meat. They looked in people's bags. They took food. They were the first thieves. Thieves are people who steal.

They got bored. They also stole toys. The girl found a piece of animal skin. She waved it in the air. She beat it with her hand. She turned it into a drum. The boy found a rock and flint. Flints are fire-starters. The boy hit the rock and flint together. He made sparks.

The main meat for Inuit is wild reindeer, or caribou.

No, my name is not Rudolph.

The party was ending. The boy said, "The sun is rising. We're going to get caught."

The girl said, "We must hide. Or we will be punished."

The boy said, "We could turn into animals."

The girl said, "I don't want to do that. Let's run away to the sky."

That's what they did. They took their toys. They fled to the sky. The girl became thunder. The boy became lightning. That's how thunder and lightning came to be.

This story is also a **cautionary** tale. Cautionary means a warning. It teaches children to behave. If they disobey, they'll turn into sky ghosts. The story also teaches children not to steal.

This story was told by mothers and grandmothers. It was told to young children.

CHAPTER 4

HOW STORMS ARE FORMED

Who is Henry Hudson?
What happened at the Catskill Mountains?
What lesson did he and his crew learn?

Tall tales are special stories. They're told as if they're true. But they're not. Henry Hudson was an English sea explorer. He explored Canada and the northeastern parts of the United States. He was a real person. But some stories about him aren't real.

In 1609, Hudson sailed his ship. His ship was named *Half Moon*. Hudson sailed into a river in New York.

He looked for a passage to Asia. He couldn't find it. So he turned his ship around. This much is true.

The river was named the Hudson River.

He stopped at the Catskill Mountains. At midnight, he heard strange sounds. He took a team of sailors. Hudson and his men went toward the sounds. They stood on a mountaintop. They looked down. They saw something amazing.

They saw gnomes. Gnomes are magical beings. They're little people. They have long, bushy beards. They have dark, beady eyes. They were dancing. They were singing. They were making music. They were doing this around a fire. They saw Hudson and his men. They invited them to their party. They pulled them close to their fire. They fed them. They gave them drinks. Hudson was the only one who didn't drink.

Their favorite game was bowling. They played all night. Each time they rolled the ball, thunder would shake the mountains. The fire flames created lightning. The gnomes sprayed their drinks. This became rain. This is how storms were made.

Hudson said, "It's getting late. We must get going. Where are my men? I can't find them."

The gnomes laughed. Hudson realized his men had turned into gnomes. He asked, "What happened?"

The leader of the gnomes said, "You drank our drinks. These drinks turn men into gnomes. They'll change back in the morning."

These gnomes were known for making things out of metal.

Hudson took his men back to the ship. He let them sleep. The men changed back. They learned their lesson. They never drank again.

Every 20 years, the ghosts of Hudson and his men returned to the Catskill Mountains. They hung out with the gnomes. They bowled. They made storms.

Another famous story set in the Catskill Mountains is about Rip Van Winkle.

DID YOU KNOW?

> Anansi is a spider. He's a trickster. Tricksters play tricks and fool others. Anansi is a popular character in West African folktales. Anansi visited the Sky God. The Sky God liked Anansi. He gave him the power to spin. Many Anansi stories explain how and why things came to be. Anansi stories became Aunt Nancy and Brer Rabbit of the American South. Many African Americans living there came from people who were taken from the western coast of Africa.

> Native American stories are different from European stories. European stories are based on the number three. There are stories of three sisters and stories of three wishes. Three is based on the Christian religion. It represents the Father, Son, and Holy Spirit. Native American stories focus on the number four. There are four winds: north, south, east, and west. There are four seasons. Native Americans focus on nature.

CHALLENGE:

WRITE YOUR OWN TALE

BEFORE YOU WRITE:

❯ Read other pourquoi tales. Read tales from different cultures. Use these tales as models.

❯ Decide the topic of your pourquoi tale. Think of things in nature. Examples are animals, places, and weather. Research these things. Ask yourself, "What is odd about this?"

❯ Brainstorm how and why things came to be. Make a list of ideas.

AS YOU WRITE:

❯ Start with the line: "A long time ago …"

❯ Describe the setting. Tell when and where the tale takes place.

❯ Describe the characters. Consider including talking animals. Don't name the characters.

❯ Set the scene for the way things were before the change.

❯ Describe the problem.

❯ Explain how the character solves the problem. Show the character's traits.

❯ End the tale describing the change. The change is usually the title. The title starts with "How" or "Why."

❯ Include a lesson. Describe what the character learns.

AFTER YOU WRITE:

❯ Proofread and edit your tale.

❯ Keep the story short. Cut details as needed.

❯ Make sure your pourquoi tale explains something. Does it explain how things came to be? Does it explain why certain things act in a certain way? Does it explain how a certain thing looks?

❯ Make sure your tale teaches a lesson.

❯ Share your story with others. Add details for each telling. See how the story continues to change.

❯ Have several people write pourquoi stories about the same topic. Compare how they're the same. Compare how they're different.

CONSIDER THIS!

TAKE A POSITION! People wonder. They want to know why. They get answers from science. Or they get answers from stories. What is more important: stories or science? Argue your point with reasons and evidence.

SAY WHAT? Read the 45th Parallel Press book about creation tales. Explain how creation tales and pourquoi tales are the same. Explain how they're different.

THINK ABOUT IT! Find out the science behind one of the stories in this book. Do research. Make connections between the science and the story. As a challenge, write your own pourquoi story about the topic.

LEARN MORE!

Hamilton, Martha, and Mitch Weiss. *How & Why Stories*. Little Rock, AR: August House Publishers, 1999.

Kipling, Rudyard. *Just So Stories*. London: Macmillan Classics, 2015.

Mayo, Margaret. *When the World Was Young: Creation and Pourquoi Tales*. New York: Simon & Schuster Books for Young Readers, 1996.

GLOSSARY

brag (BRAG) to show off

brer (BRAIR) brother

cautionary (KAW-shuhn-er-ee) a warning

creator (kree-AY-tur) a supreme being that created the world

dam (DAM) a barrier that holds back water

flint (FLINT) a hard gray rock that is used with steel to start fires

gnomes (NOMEZ) little people that are magical beings

orphans (OR-funz) children whose parents have died

pourquoi (por-QWAH) French word meaning "why"

slaves (SLAYVZ) people stolen from their homes and forced to work

tall tales (TAL TAYLZ) exaggerated stories that are told as if they're true but are not true

thieves (THEEVZ) people who commit a crime by stealing

upright (UHP-rite) sitting or standing vertically or erect with a straight back

INDEX